Common Sense Ain't Common

A guide for positioning yourself to take full advantage of your credit and financial opportunities!

by

H. Shane Darrisaw

authorHOUSE®

AuthorHouse™
1663 Liberty Drive, Suite 200
Bloomington, IN 47403
www.authorhouse.com
Phone: 1-800-839-8640

First published by AuthorHouse 4/7/2008

ISBN: 978-1-4343-7559-9 (sc)

Library of Congress Control Number: 2008902210

Printed in the United States of America
Bloomington, Indiana

This book is printed on acid-free paper.

Dedication

I dedicate this book to Yvette Darrisaw (my wife) and Trey Justin Darrisaw (our son). Both of you are my inspiration and the reasons why I wake up every morning ready to take on the world.

To my wife:

I thank God for you because he knew before I did what I needed in a wife and delivered that to me. Thank you for telling me that I think I know everything, which is partly the inspiration for writing this book! For the record, I do not think I know everything but I do know how deep my love is for you!

To our son:

Trey, you are my claim! In you I see a boy that is happy, full of energy and enthusiasm. You have inherited a rich heritage from every Darrisaw man before you! You are destined to be a great man of integrity and achievement, and I look forward to witnessing you become that man. You should know that Daddy will always love you and be there for you no matter what!

Table of Contents

Acknowledgements

Hubert and Wylene Darrisaw (my mother and father)

Thank you both for raising me to believe that I can accomplish anything. Thank you for instilling in me the spirit of achievement. Thank you for building in me an "I can" philosophy. I love you because you sacrificed so much for all of your children.

Anissa, Stacey and Gregory Darrisaw (my sisters and brother)

As your big brother, I have always tried to set the example of what a big brother should be. When we were growing up, I know I was overprotective and gave you advice when you thought you did not need it. Thank you for listening anyway. I love you all!

Earl Moore and John Little

Earl, you recruited me for the position that allowed me to pursue my passion, and you challenged me to grow that passion. Now you mentor me when I need to be mentored. John, you don't know this but when you wrote your book, you actually forced me to stop *talking* and start *walking*! The bible reads "... as iron sharpens iron, so does one man sharpen another" (Proverbs 27:17). Thank you both for sharpening me!

Introduction

Why would anyone want to write a book about common sense, proclaiming that everyone does not have it? In my life of 41 years, I have met hundreds of people of varying education levels and of all professions. I have friends who are doctors, engineers, attorneys, educators, bankers and a few that possess doctorates in fields from education to psychology. One thing I can say about all of them is that I have from time to time seen occasions where they did not exercise common sense.

I too have been accused of not using common sense when it comes to certain situations, so I include myself in this number and by no means intend to offend anyone. Rather, I am taking this opportunity for self-healing (they say the first step towards recovery is admission).

I am writing this book because I believe that this book can help anyone who wants help, by sharing my thoughts in the area of financial awareness mixed with a little bit of the lessons taught by life.

This book is my perspective on what it takes to start the wealth-building process for you and the ones you love. If I speak on anything that helps you, then I will consider the book a success. If, on the other hand, you do not find anything in this book helpful, then you should consider yourself in the minority and one of the fortunate ones that exercises common sense all of the time because ...

Common sense ain't common. If it were, everyone would use it!

CHAPTER 1

We Are All a Sum Total of Our Life's Experiences

The inspiration behind this book comes from the things I have learned in my life from childhood to college, from the U.S. military, my professional career, becoming a father and, most of all, from my marriage. In other words, the choices we make in life shape who we are — thus the statement that we are all a sum total of our life's experiences. How can life's experiences help you financially?

- Mistakes of the past concerning our finances do not have to be repeated if you take heed and embrace the lessons learned in failing.

- If you knew then what you know now, you might still have failed. However, you would have failed better.

- The common mistakes we make concerning our finances.

- Emotional decisions concerning finances versus rational decisions and the difference between the two.

- What should common sense teach us concerning our finances and the early stages of adulthood?

These are the issues and questions that will be addressed in this chapter.

I landed a full-time job three months prior to graduating from college on the condition that I was a college grad by my start date, which was early July. Imagine that. Here I was in 1989, just 22 years old, and already I had lined up a full-time job ready and waiting upon my graduation. I was on top of the world.

Since I was on top of the world, I acted accordingly and applied for credit cards from Visa, MasterCard and American Express as well as going out and getting myself a brand new, fully loaded 1990 Nissan Pulsar. I also signed a two-year lease on a very nice apartment (bachelor pad) in the city where my job was located. Oh, I forgot to mention that I had student loans I had to start repaying six months after graduation, as well as all of the expenses that go along with relocating, establishing a new residence, buying a work wardrobe and all of the ignorance that goes along with being a new college grad and, as my dad would say, "a grown man now." To make my point about this very painful story, here is how I ended up just three short months after graduation.

I overextended myself on all three credit cards, buying whatever I wanted using whatever card that was accepted at the store I was in at the time!

I missed the first three payments on my brand new car and was parking my car in a different spot each night when I got home just in case the bank was out to repossess it.

I had a notice on my apartment door asking me to pay in full the past-due rent or I would face eviction.

So here is what I learned from my mistakes, because as I stated earlier, mistakes of the past concerning our finances do not have to be repeated if you take heed and embrace the lesson learned in failing.

Lesson learned: be frugal in times of prosperity.

If you knew then what you know now, you might still have failed. However, you would have failed better.

Merriam-Webster's Collegiate Dictionary defines failure as **"(noun) nonperformance of something due, required, or expected."**

As I stated earlier, I landed a full-time job before I graduated college. I was a buyer at one of the largest retail stores in the nation. My specific responsibility was as a buyer for the children's, shoe and home furnishings departments. My job was to purchase items for those departments that would generate a sales profit over and above the assigned sales goal and over last year's numbers. This position sounds exciting and challenging right? What it actually meant was that I had to manage 20 people all older than me, watch hours of video tape sent from the corporate office and make purchase orders based on what I thought would sell and exceed the departments' goals. I was visited by potential vendors, all trying to sell me their products. All I had to do was "make the right decision every time," to quote my boss at the time.

I was working six days a week, and when I had the weekend off, I had to fulfill my military obligation as an officer in the U.S. Army Reserve, which was one weekend a month and two weeks in the summer months, as well as additional training that was required for continuing education and promotion. By my own admission, I was failing miserably at my job, and I was not making enough money to fulfill my monthly obligations. In other words, I hated the life I was living because this was the first time that I had experienced failure as an adult. I knew something had to change because I did not want failure to be part of my future.

The next day I made a decision. I decided that I would give my current job one year to see if it was the right job for me and to see if I could turn my financial situation around. I had been on the job for 97 days, which meant I had 268 days to turn things around or to quit and move on to something more promising.

I made a commitment to contact all of my creditors and tell them my situation (that I was overextended and that I was going to pay my debts if they would work with me). Surprisingly, all of them understood and did just that. They allowed me to establish a payment plan to catch up on all of my debts, as long as I kept in contact with them and updated them on my situation on a weekly basis. In my mind I was still failing, but at least I was failing better. I was failing better because I had learned that I could not put my wants before my financial obligations. I also learned that, for me, debt was like a form of slavery that keeps you chained to despair and that if you allow it to, it will consume you.

If I knew then what I know now, I still would have accepted the job I was offered, but I would have kept my 1984 Dodge Colt with no a/c, I would not have applied for any credit cards and I would have stayed in the apartment I had with my college buddies until I had adequate savings. This would have afforded me the right mindset to focus on my job and allowed me to perform at a high level while gaining valuable experience. I still gained valuable experience, but it was one of the toughest lessons I have ever learned. I did, however, keep the commitment I made to myself — on the 365th day of my job, I quit because there had to be a better way for me. I did not know what I was going to do, but I knew I was not going to continue the downward spiral.

Lesson learned: consider times of adversity as character building experiences.

By now, I am 22 years old, unemployed and dreading the fact that I was going to have to move back in with my parents because, except for the income generated from being in the Army Reserve, I had no money. Here are some common mistakes we make concerning our finances — or at least here are the mistakes I made concerning my finances:

- I did not establish a budget.

- I had no savings to fall back on.

- I quit my job without having another one lined up.

- I did not know what I wanted to do with my education or how to apply it.

- I forgot that when I quit my job, I still had financial obligations that had to be met.

Not establishing a budget, with a savings plan and other contingencies for emergencies, is a mistake that every day a lot of people make. Quitting your job before you have another one is just stupid. I was reminded of just how stupid it was every time one of my creditors would contact me concerning my obligation.

Lesson learned: business has no friends, no heart and does not care for excuses.

Up until this point, all of the decisions I made were based on emotion instead of on rational thought. By this I mean I made decisions based on how I felt or how tired I was or what I felt like when I woke up. I learned that I should be making my decisions based on facts and substance. Rational thinking leads to sound decisions that yield long-lasting positive results. Emotional decisions may be satisfying temporarily, but like anything temporary, the satisfaction is gone before you know it. So what is the lesson here? Emotional decisions are for affairs of the heart. Rational decisions are for business, because if you cannot take care of business in a rational manner, business will take care of you. Then you will have to deal with the emotions of depression, sadness, despair and anger.

Lesson learned: the difference between rational decisions and emotional decisions; decisions concerning finances should be based on rational thought.

What does common sense teach us concerning our finances and the early stages of adulthood? Here is what it taught me!

Be frugal

Simply put, be wise when it comes to all of your expenditures, big and small. Save and spend sparingly and to the extent possible, incur few long-term expenses unless they are investments that yield a positive return.

Consider times of adversity as character-building experiences

As we all grow older, one thing is inevitable — you will face challenging times. Those that endure are made stronger as a result of the experience. Those that do not endure see the world in a totally negative light. Show me anyone you admire or consider as having it "made" in life, and I will show you someone who has endured adversity. The character that is formed as a result of adversity is the trait that got them to where they are today!

Business has no friends

The sole purpose of business is to generate profit. It does not matter who is negatively impacted by the profit generated just as long as a profit is made. Business decisions are made every day in meetings we never witness or hear about that serve no other purpose than to squeeze every penny of profit out of the operating model. You shouldn't take this personally because if you are ever negatively impacted by business, the explanation you will get is "Don't take it personally, it's just business"!

Make decisions concerning finances based on rational thought

This is truly self-explanatory. Rational thought leads to rational decisions. Rational decisions lead to solid results.

NOTES

CHAPTER 2

Credit Grantors:
Financial Institutions and
Human Institutions

After dating for a couple of years the woman that was to be my wife, I decided to ask for her hand in marriage. I thought long and hard of how I was going to pop the question. I figured that before I asked her to be my wife, it would be a good idea to seek the counsel of her father and get his blessing. Since I was raised in the South and taught by my father the rules of how a man is supposed to act when he realizes he is a man, I decided that this was the best course of action just in case he had some issues with me as a man and as the husband of his daughter.

I called my future father-in-law's house and asked if I could stop by after church that Sunday. I thought this was a good day and time because it was football season and I lived in St. Louis at the time. The Rams had not lost a game yet and they were on their way to the Super Bowl. I also knew that, like most men, he would be paying more attention to the game and not to the conversation we were having (brilliant, huh). My timing was perfect! When the Rams were on a scoring drive, I started in on my conversation. I told him I loved his daughter and I wanted to marry her. He was silent. I thought, this can't be good. He turned the television off and looked at me. He said, "So you want to marry my daughter?" I said "yes" with confidence. He said, "You seem like a nice enough fellow and I know you've been in the military for some time, plus I hear you have a good reputation on your job and I like you." I responded with, "I like you as well." He then said, "All of that is fine and dandy, but do you know that marriage is the ultimate commitment? ... Are you ready for that type of commitment?" I replied again with a very confident "yes," but this time I looked him in the eyes. He floored me with the next question. "How is your credit?"

I thought to myself, what in the world does my credit have to do with marrying your daughter? What came out of my mouth was, "Excuse me?" He said, "How is your credit?" I responded with, "I can't see how that is any of your business," but I ended this statement with "sir" to show respect. He leaned forward and said in a stern voice, "If you call yourself a man then you must take care of your responsibilities. Taking on a wife does not relieve you of that responsibility; in fact, it only increases that responsibility." He went on and on for about five minutes. He paused for a second and made the most profound statement to me. He said, "If Visa, MasterCard or Discover will not accept your last name because your credit is bad, then why should my daughter?" I sat back and thought to myself, he is right. I paused for a second and then leaned forward with my hand on my chin.

I responded with, "Sir, I assure you that my credit is fine. In fact, I have been looking at houses with plans of having one built after I asked your daughter to marry me and she said yes." He responded, "If you have your financial affairs in order and you meet your obligations on time, then you are okay by me. I would love to have you as a son-in-law." I responded with a confident "Thank you for your blessing." He replied, "Now you have to go ask her mother."

My father-in-law didn't know it at the time, but the exercise he put me through is something I remember to this very day, and I always laugh about it. The statement he made is how you are seen in corporate America. It is also a great indicator of character.

Your credit is a reflection of your character, ability and willingness to satisfy your financial obligations. Therefore, if you meet your financial obligations, you have the ability to understand the concept of the marriage commitment. He taught me a lesson that day as well.

Lesson learned: your credit is a reflection of you, and financial institutions will treat you according to this reflection. Good credit equals good character.

Human institutions (also known as people) judge your character or credit on a totally different scale. People often judge you based on first impressions or, as they say, they judge a book by its cover. The problem with this is that the first impression you give may not be an accurate reflection, since it is based on the circumstances you are faced with when having that first-impression encounter. The cover may not tell the reader that you are a best seller wrapped in shreds.

Whatever the case, human institutions make the mistake every day of judging other individuals and being wrong in their judgment. The reason for this error in judgment is really quite simple. We should not judge others at all. Rather, we should believe in the good in people unless they show us otherwise. In other words, when people show you who and what they are, you should believe them. We could all take a lesson from the FICO credit-scoring model to some extent. At least it judges you based on your past or a snapshot of facts concerning your credit. Humans either give you too much credit or not enough credit for your past deeds.

When you give an individual too much or too little credit, quite often you are doing so because of the superficial or external. This gives the individual in question an opportunity to do one of three things (disappointment, infatuation or idolizing). There are two potential outcomes and neither of these outcomes is fair to the individual.

When you give an individual too much credit, you stand the risk of being disappointed. This occurs because you gave credit before it was earned. You can be taken advantage of by the individual and suffer grave consequences as a result. These consequences may not be reparable and may discredit you as well. Be careful not to give a person too much credit.

When you give an individual too little credit, you stand the risk of underestimating that person's true potential. This occurs because you believe they have no value or little that they can offer. When you do not give credit to a person when it is deserved, the individual in question will sense this and it could be a blow to their self-esteem. Be careful not to give a person too little credit.

Ideally, we should all remember that we all share the same space and that the world is a big place. None of us should focus too much on judging others because we never know when or where we will need them.

Lesson learned: when people show you who and what they are, believe them.

What does common sense teach us concerning credit? Here is what it has taught me!

Concerning credit

A person's credit should be closely guarded, for it is the best indicator of a person's character in the business world. The credit-scoring model was formulated over 50 years ago by the Fair Isaac Corporation (FICO).

Credit scores are used to make decisions concerning everything from home ownership to automobile purchases to homeowner insurance and even employment opportunities. So do your level best to maintain good credit.

Judging others

Judge not lest ye be judged.

NOTES

CHAPTER 3

Credit History

Your credit history is a reflection of your character. This is the way those in the financial or credit industry view you. It is a snapshot of your financial life over a period of time. It is also an indicator of your future with respect to how you will handle your financial obligations. In short, your credit determines your station in life. This being the case, let's take a look at what I believe are the keys to establishing and maintaining excellent credit.

When most of us enter adulthood, we start out full of optimism and excitement about what life has in store for us. We believe we can accomplish anything (which is true), and we will let no one stand in our way. This being the case, you should approach your credit as the single most important responsibility you will undertake as a young adult. No other indicator shows you are an adult like good credit. Ask anyone you respect that happens to be older about establishing credit. Almost all of them will tell you that establishing good credit is the key to a stable foundation. Here are the fundamentals when establishing solid credit.

Pay your bills on time

This seems self-explanatory; however, this is apparently easier said than done. Millions of people pay their bills based on when they get paid versus paying according to the date the bill is due. Now you may be thinking, what is the problem with that? I can't pay the bill until I get paid from my job. Here is the solution. If at all possible, pay your bills with the paycheck you receive in the pay period prior to the bill's due date. For example, my mortgage payment is due on the 1st of each month. However, I pay it on the 15th of each month, thus paying that note 15 days early. I apply this same methodology to all of my other debts. I budget the expected amount of the bills I pay every month for the pay period prior to the bill coming due.

That way, when the bill comes, I pay it immediately either through snail mail or online as a debit from my checking account. Either way, I avoid late penalties and the possibility of a negative hit on my credit. Keep in mind that a late payment is any payment that is paid 30 or more days after a due date. For every day over 30, you incur a greater penalty on your credit score.

Pay off debt rather than move it around

In most cases, the practice of transferring a balance from one credit card to another does not benefit you. Per the FICO scoring model, the debt is still out there; your debt-to-income ratio has not changed just by moving it from credit card A to credit card B. By moving debt around, you may be doing further damage to your credit because of the *balance-to-limit ratio* you encounter when taking your credit card balance over a certain limit. The FICO scoring model is such that you are penalized or negatively impacted when your balance is greater than 30%, 50% or 80% of the predetermined limit. You also stand the risk of moving the balance of a more mature credit card to one that is less mature. If you are going to move the balance of one credit card to another, make sure you are moving the balance from one that is newer to one that is older. The more-established credit card has a greater weight than the newer one.

Apply for and open new credit based on needs not wants

Just because the item you want may be the hottest and latest does not justify a need for it. Often times, the store or entity offers a discount on your purchase or future purchases if you get their credit card. Consider this: the discount they offer is generally offset by the interest rate they charge; thus, they are still making a profit.

For example, you go into a clothing store offering an additional 10% off the merchandise if you get their credit card and purchase the merchandise with their credit card. However, the interest rate on the card is 24%. The item sells for $99.99 but you get an additional 10% off saving $9.99. You pay by credit card 30 days later and you pay $111.59 because you missed the interest-free period. Now had you paid cash for the item, you would have paid $99.99 plus tax, but because you got the credit card saving you 10% of the purchase price, you actually paid an additional $11.60 — all because of the perceived discount. How smart is that?

You only need one major credit card versus a variety of revolving credit cards

Most major credit cards are accepted at most places of business; therefore, any credit card offered by the store you are in does not trump your major credit card. Quite often, your major credit card has a rate that is lower or very competitive in comparison to the rate of the store's credit card, and major cards are accepted at more places. The store credit card is only accepted at that store and it is human nature to charge it to the limit because of the ease of use. This again plays with the balance-to-limit ratio on your credit score, possibly driving your credit score down.

Keep balances low on credit cards and other revolving credit

Now let's go into a little more detail concerning the balance-to-limit ratio when discussing revolving credit. Revolving credit is accounted for differently than installment credit. With an installment balance, the payment applied to the balance reduces the balance by the amount of the payment, assuming there are no late charges. On a revolving account, the payment made on your balance reduces the balance by that amount less the next period's finance charge, thus applying a portion towards the balance and a portion towards the new finance charge.

It takes much longer to pay off the balance, and you stand the risk of having a balance greater than 30%, 50% or 80% of the limit, which negatively impacts your credit. If at all possible, try to keep your revolving credit balances at or below 30% of the limit established.

Protect yourself from identity theft

In this day and age, it is very easy for someone to steal your identity. By this I mean that someone can steal your good credit history, your medical records or your driving license information. If this happens to you, it will be a challenge trying to undo everything the thief has done. In addition, you will often be treated as the thief (until you prove otherwise) as a result of this happening to you, which is not a pleasant experience. Here are your legal rights concerning identity theft, according to my research and experience as well as my own common sense.

You have the right to:

- File a report with a law enforcement agency and ask for a copy of it to show how your identity has been misused. This report is often called a police report.

An identity theft report is a second kind of report. It is a police report with more detail. To be an identity theft report, it should have enough information about the crime that the credit reporting companies and the businesses involved can verify that you're a victim, and know which accounts or information have been affected. It's the report that will give you access to many of the rights described here.

It is also a good idea to file an ID theft complaint form with the FTC. This form asks you for the kind of detail that the identity theft report requires. Once you fill out this form, you can use it with the police report to create your identity theft report.

Dealing with Credit Reporting Companies

You have the right to:

- Place a 90-day initial fraud alert on your credit files. You would do this if you think you are — or may become — the victim of identity theft. A fraud alert tells users of your credit report that they must take reasonable steps to verify who is applying for credit in your name. To place a 90-day fraud alert, contact just one credit reporting companies (Equifax, Transunion or Experian). The one you contact has to notify the other two.

- Place a seven-year extended fraud alert on your credit files. You would do this if you know you are a victim of identity theft. You will need to give an identity theft report to each of the credit reporting companies. Each credit reporting company will ask you to give them some way for potential creditors to reach you, like a phone number. They will place this contact information on the extended fraud alert as a signal to those who use your credit report that they must contact you before they can issue credit in your name.

- Obtain a free copy of your credit report and a summary of your rights from each credit reporting company. You can get these when you place a 90-day initial fraud alert on your credit reports. When you place an extended fraud alert with any credit reporting company, you have the right to two copies of that credit report during a 12-month period. These credit reports are in addition to the free credit report that all consumers are entitled to each year.

- Ask the credit reporting companies to block fraudulent information from appearing on your credit report. To do this, you must submit a copy of your identity theft report. The credit reporting companies then must tell any creditors who gave them fraudulent information that it resulted from identity theft. The creditors may not then turn the fraudulent debts over to debt collectors.

- Dispute fraudulent or inaccurate information on your credit report with a credit reporting company. The credit reporting company must investigate your charges, and fix your report if they find that the information is fraudulent.

In many states, you have the right to restrict access to your credit report through a credit freeze. A credit freeze makes it more difficult for an identity thief to open a new account in your name. Your state attorney general's office has information about using a credit freeze where you live.

Dealing with Creditors, Debt Collectors, and Merchants

You have the right to:

- Have a credit report free of fraudulent accounts. Once you give creditors and debt collectors a copy of a valid identity theft report, they may not report fraudulent accounts to the credit reporting companies.

- Get copies of documents related to the theft of your identity — for example, applications used to open new accounts or transaction records — if you give the company a valid police report. You also can tell the company to give the documents to a specific law enforcement agency; that agency doesn't have to get a subpoena for the records.

- Stop the collection of fraudulent debts. You may ask debt collectors to stop contacting you to collect on fraudulent debts. You also may ask them to give you information related to the debt, like the names of the creditors and the amounts of the debts.

In many states, you have the right to be notified by a business or organization that has lost or misplaced certain types of personal information. Contact your state attorney general's office for more information.

Limiting Your Loss from Identity Theft

Various laws limit your liability for fraudulent debts caused by identity theft.

- Fraudulent Credit Card Charges: You cannot be held liable for more than $50 for fraudulent purchases made with your credit card, as long as you let the credit card company know within 60 days of when the credit card statement with the fraudulent charges was sent to you. Some credit card issuers say cardholders who are victims of fraudulent transactions on their accounts have no liability for them at all.

- Lost or stolen ATM/Debit Card: If your ATM or debit card is lost or stolen, you may not be held liable for more than $50 for the misuse of your card, as long as you notify the bank or credit union within two business days after you realize the card is missing. If you do not report the loss of your card promptly, your liability may increase.

- Fraudulent Electronic Withdrawals: If fraudulent electronic withdrawals are made from your bank or credit union account, and your ATM or debit card has not been lost or stolen, you are not liable, as long as you notify the bank or credit union in writing of the error within 60 days of the date the bank or credit union account statement with the fraudulent withdrawals was sent to you.

- Fraudulent Checks: Under most state laws, you are liable for just a limited amount for fraudulent checks issued on your bank or credit union account, as long as you notify the bank or credit union promptly. Contact your state banking or consumer protection agency for more information.

- Fraudulent New Accounts: Under most state laws, you are not liable for any debt incurred on fraudulent accounts opened in your name and without your permission. Contact your state attorney general's office for more information.

Other Federal Rights

Identity theft victims have other rights when the identity thief is being prosecuted in federal court. For example, under the Justice for All Act, the U.S. Department of Justice says identity theft victims have the right:

- to be reasonably protected from the accused; to reasonable, accurate, and timely notice of any public court proceeding, any parole proceeding involving the crime, or any release or escape of the accused;

- to not be excluded from any such public court proceeding unless the court determines that the identity theft victim's testimony would be materially altered if he or she heard other testimony at that proceeding;

- to be reasonably heard at any public proceeding in the district court involving release, plea, sentencing, or any parole proceeding;

- to confer with the attorney for the government in the case;

- to full and timely restitution as provided in law;

- to proceedings free from unreasonable delay; and

- to be treated with fairness and with respect for his or her dignity and privacy.

What does common sense teach us about our credit history? Here is what it taught me.

Your credit history should be safeguarded

Shred all documents that have your Social Security number, account info or any other information that will allow someone to steal your identity.

Review a copy of your credit report every 6 to 12 months

Look for inaccuracies and accounts that do not belong to you as well as any other errors concerning your credit. This way you can contact the creditor directly to inquire, before damage is done.

Learn your rights

The FTC as well as all three credit reporting agencies have websites that contain information on your rights concerning identity theft, so take advantage of it!

Cosigning on loans

You should be careful not to cosign on any loan or apply for a credit card jointly unless it is for a spouse or a young adult son or daughter. I would really like to say that you should never cosign for anyone; however, there are circumstances when you may want to help your spouse, son or daughter establish or reestablish credit. Proceed with caution because as cosigner, you are equally responsible for the debt incurred!

NOTES

CHAPTER 4

Success Before Work

My father has always been my idol because he did not mind working. As an adult, he served full-time in the Army and Navy during the Korean War, finishing his 20-year military career in the Navy Reserve. Still a young man, he went to work for the United States Post Office, serving another 20 years before retiring from that. Several times as a child I remember my father picking up a part-time job when he was not working at the post office, running his newspaper route or being a handyman and shade tree mechanic. One day he asked me what I wanted to be when I grew up. I replied that I wanted to be a postman, like him. He got upset and put me on punishment and told me to go to my room (but not before tapping me on the behind). Later, he came into my room and said, "Son, you do not want to be a postman and work for the U.S. Post Office. I want you want to do better than me. I want you to go to college and be whatever you aspire to be as long as you do not mind working for it!"

I knew he was serious because he was looking me in the eye and pointing his finger at me. He followed up that statement with, "I want you to work hard and be successful … The only place you can find success before work is in the dictionary." He was right! S comes before W in the alphabet and in the dictionary. My father was not mad at me as I thought he was at the time. Rather, he did not want me to have to struggle as he had done to provide for his family. He wanted me to get an education and really apply myself, to strive for success and make him proud because I put forth the effort. The rest of this chapter talks about the lessons he taught me and how common sense saved me from a different path.

Weed killer

This story is not about what you think it is about. You see, my dad was old-fashioned or, as they say, *old school*. Each Saturday he would go out and mow the lawn. Up until about the age of ten, I would just sit in the house and watch him through the window. One day he came in hot and sweaty and asked me if I wanted to help. I was happy because I thought I was finally going to get my chance to push the lawnmower. My dad had a different idea in mind. He wanted me to get the weeds up in the yard. Back then, pesticide weed killers weren't as prominent as they are today. Back then, you had to dig the weeds up with a forklike utensil I called a *spatula*. This was time-consuming and tedious work because we had a big yard and a billion weeds. Every time I would dig one up, I swear another would grow in its place as soon as I turned my back. I would have to dig weeds up every week, and it would take all day. My dad would finish mowing the lawn in about 45 minutes, but it would take me several hours to dig up the weeds.

Raking the leaves

In our backyard, we had three big beautiful pecan trees. My brother and I loved to play in the backyard and pick pecans to eat while we rested. When I was old enough, my dad would make me rake the leaves that had fallen from the pecan trees. Did I mention we had a big backyard? This was again an all-day task, and my brother, who is six years younger than I, was considered too young to help or would not stay focused on the task at hand long enough to be of any significant use. I noticed one thing when raking leaves — the wind would always blow. This made it very frustrating, since I wanted to play. I would rake the leaves into a pile, and the wind would blow them back to their place of origin scattered on the ground. One day I went into the house mad and asked my dad why I had to rake the leaves so often when all that would happen is the wind would blow more leaves on the ground from the pecan trees.

I said this with such frustration that my dad could only laugh and told me to come into the house, which got me out of raking leaves every day. Now I only had to rake leaves every *other* day.

Cleaning the tires

Another thing my dad did on the weekends was wash the car and the truck. He would let me help, but he would only let me do the tires. This doesn't seem so bad, right? I would agree with you if it weren't for the fact that these were white wall tires, which I think are obsolete now, so be happy. My dad would wash the car and the truck in about 30 minutes each and would hand me a bucket and a Brillo Pad. You may not recognize a Brillo Pad, but it was similar to steel wool. My dad would expect me to clean the white wall tires until they were white, because he and my mom liked a clean car and a clean car wasn't clean if the white wall tires had even a smudge of dirt. Because of the experience, to this day I get anxious when I see white wall tires.

Cutting the grass

When I became of age, my father finally let me mow the lawn all by myself, and I was happy he let me because I was promoted from weed killer duty and that duty was passed on to my brother. Only one stipulation: I had to cut the front and back yard on Saturday before my dad got home from work. I had to do this while my friends were playing and picking at me because the yard was so big. They would say, "How much is your dad paying you for all of this work." Or "After you mow the lawn, please put the goal post up so we can play football." I have mentioned that we had a big yard, but did I also mention that I was raised in central Georgia and it was always hot? That did not matter to my dad. We had an understanding that the yard had better be mowed by the time he got home. If not, there would be consequences and repercussions to deal with.

Boxing with dear old Dad

About once a week, my dad would walk right in front of me and asked me to stand up and put up my fists. I knew what was coming next; he wanted me to protect myself because he was going to spar with me. This started when I was about 12 years old and did not stop until I was about 15. Each time, he would start off tapping me softly, but as it progressed, he would hit me harder and harder while my mom looked on, fearing that I would get hurt or get a tooth knocked out. This would go on for about five minutes and always ended up with me taking a shot to the lip, my lip swelling up and me running to my room crying. My dad would say, "Stop running and fight back." Eventually, I got mad and tired of being hit, so I started hitting him as hard as I could in the stomach. I would do this because he always protected his face, so if I wanted to end the match, I had to hit him in the stomach — hard! Eventually, it got to the point where I would ask him to box and I would immediately hit him as hard as I could in the stomach, which would send him to the floor. I would then say, "Stop running and fight back." He soon grew tired of me sucker punching him and stopped asking me to box.

Now you may wonder what these short stories of my childhood have to do with common sense and success before work. Well here is what it taught me:

- Digging up weeds by hand taught me to be thorough.

- Raking leaves taught me organization.

- Cleaning the tires taught me to be meticulous with my work.

- Mowing the lawn taught me how to do backwards planning.

- Boxing with dad taught me how to stand up for myself.

Let me explain!

Digging up weeds

Attention to detail or being thorough is taught to individuals in many different ways. For me, digging up weeds in the front yard taught me that if I am going to start a task, then I should see it through to completion. This lesson learned would prove vital over the years. I have been told that I am now a very thorough person when embarking on a task whether it is for work or personal gain. I guess I always think of digging up weeds when I am working on a task and the thought of the weeds growing back if I do not dig them up by the root drives me to make sure that I am thorough! An example of this is when I found an error on my credit report. In order to ensure the error was removed from my credit, I had to be thorough with my follow-through and I had to make sure I had everyone's names and positions and every little detail of our conversations, to help expedite the process.

Raking leaves

Organization should be the foundation of every task we set out to complete. If there is no organization, then chaos will rule. When I raked leaves, I learned that in order to get this done efficiently and still be able to play with my friends, I had to be organized. I knew I needed a rake and trash bags to put leaves in, and I knew I had to start raking from the perimeter and work my way around in a circular motion. If I did this with no organization, it would take me twice as long to complete the task. I would spend more of my time working rather than playing. Organization is also key when handling your finances and budgeting. If your finances are not organized, then your finances are in control of you instead of the other way around. Organizing your finances keeps you from being a slave to debt.

Cleaning the tires

Meticulous by definition means taking or showing extreme care about minute details. In other words, to be fussy or finicky! Because my dad only allowed me to clean the tires when he was washing cars, I knew that if I wanted to do more than the tires (meaning wash the car itself), I had to do a meticulous job with the tires. This carried over into how I manage my finances and credit. In order to obtain and maintain a high credit score, I knew I had to be meticulous when it came to managing my credit. I learned that in order to keep a FICO score of 750 or better, I could not have a lot of revolving debt. I learned that I did not need more than one credit card. I learned that I needed to do my level best not to be 30 days past due on any debt. Finally, I learned that if I did not want to be a slave to credit, I had to pay cash for the things I wanted whenever possible or do without.

Mowing the lawn

Mowing the lawn taught me how not to be late to events or appearances. This chore proved to me that backwards planning is an essential key to managing your credit and finances. Once I figured out how long it would take me to mow the lawn, I knew exactly what I needed to do and how much more I could do. Is this a confusing statement? Let me put it a different way. It took me 45 minutes to mow the lawn. My dad would get home, on average, around 3:30 p.m. from work. I found out that by backwards planning I could start mowing the lawn by 2:30 p.m. and be completely finished by 3:15 p.m., with 15 minutes to spare. When my dad got home, he would ask me if I mowed the lawn in the morning like he told me to, and I would simply reply that I did. This allowed me to goof off and watch my favorite shows on television and still complete my chores and avoid punishment. While in college, I used backwards planning to organize my studies, plan class projects and to get the most out of my day.

Today I use backwards planning in my professional career and, most recently, in meeting my self-imposed deadline for completing this book so I could start on the next one! Backwards planning is also a good concept when paying your bills.

If a bill is due on 10th and you know it takes three business days for mail to reach its destination (in most cases) and it takes one day for it to make it from the mail room to the processing room, then you should drop your payment in the mail no later than the 5th (assuming that day is a Monday and not a holiday) to make sure the payment is posted by the 9th and not considered late.

Boxing with Dad

Now boxing with Dad was a painful lesson until I got the message. My dad wanted me to stand up for myself even if I was intimidated or felt anxiety. He knew that if he could show me how to stand up to life's challenges and look them in the eye and prove I was not afraid, then I could win against the odds. Now my dad did not want me to be a violent person, but he did want me to defend myself. He wanted me to use knowledge to defend myself. I will make my point in a different way. When I first graduated from college, I bought me a brand new car and immediately got behind on the payments. I didn't call the bank for fear they would repossess the car. For this illustration, the bank represents my dad asking me to stand up and defend myself. My not wanting to call the bank represents me not wanting to get hit (get my car repossessed). By standing up for myself, I owned up to my responsibility and fought back by calling the bank and working out a plan to get caught up on a past-due debt.

In this crazy analogy, I stood up for myself by being responsible and took the initiative from then on by calling my creditors at the first sign of trouble.

I would like to thank my dad for making me dig up weeds (teaching me to be thorough), making me rake leaves (teaching me organization), making me clean the tires (teaching me to be meticulous), making me mow the lawn (teaching me to practice backwards planning) and finally for the boxing lessons (teaching me how to stand up for myself). You have taught me more than you will ever know! Success comes from the work that you do and not the pay or status you get from the work!

NOTES

CHAPTER 5

Financial Opportunities

Opportunities of a lifetime have to be seized during the lifetime of the opportunity. This is something my mother would say to all of us as we were growing up. This statement is appropriate in all cases where opportunities arise and even more so when it comes to financial opportunities. The challenge with this statement is in recognizing financial opportunities. As we grow older, most of us in most cases use past experiences to make present and future decisions. Now if you read that last statement carefully, you will notice that the phrase was "most of us in most cases." This phrase is important because it makes the point of this entire chapter. I would like to focus on the financial opportunities that come before us from time to time and how we sometimes fail to seize them.

Financial opportunity #1

Pay yourself first. How easy is this rule? Apparently it is more difficult than most of us think. When you speak with any financial planner, they will tell you how important it is to manage your money. You should know where your money is going and be able to account for every single penny. If you can account for every penny, then you should consider setting aside 10% to 15% of your gross income. Now, you may be wondering why I said 10% to 15% of your gross income and not of your net income. The answer is really quite simple: you deserve gross (all of your savings) and not net (after-tax savings). This does not apply to what goes into Company 401k, IRA or other investment vehicles. I am merely stating that you should do your level best to have at least a money market savings account, a 401k or IRA account and another investment vehicle such as a life insurance annuity or long-term investment account. Here is the philosophy behind this savings strategy and my thoughts on what makes common sense.

Your overall savings goal should be a minimum of 10% to 15% of your gross income and the breakdown should look something like this. Deposit up to the amount your company will match into your 401k. For example, if your company will match 100% of your pretax earnings up to 5%, then you should take advantage of the full benefit. In this example, let's use an income of $100,000. This means that in a calendar year you would put $5,000 into the 401k and your company would make the same commitment of $5,000 for a total calendar year savings of $10,000. Now let's talk about the money market savings account, which is better than a conventional savings account because a money market savings account shares some of the same characteristics as a money market fund. Like other savings accounts, money market accounts are FDIC (Federal Deposit Insurance Corporation) insured up to $100,000. They offer many of the same services as checking accounts although there are limits on transactions. The accounts are usually managed by banks or brokerages and can be a convenient place to store money that is earmarked for investments. Money market accounts are very safe and offer more liquidity as well as higher interest rate earnings than a conventional savings account.

Financial opportunity #2

Make wise choices with your 401k, pension and other employee investments. As you mature in the workforce, it is inevitable that you will experience employment maturity as well. By this I mean that you will change jobs several times before you find your passion or your passion finds you. During this transition from working a nine-to-five to working your passion, you will have or should have opted to take part in your company's 401k, pension, stock, and so on. As you grow and move on to other positions at other companies, you will find you have to decide what to do with your balances on previous company investments. My advice to you is to roll it over into an IRA or another investment vehicle that does not penalize you for doing so, as opposed to cashing out and spending the money. The reason is really simple. You incur a tax penalty for cashing out your investments in most cases, and the money is usually spent on something that has no future value. Here is a quick example, and I will use myself to illustrate my point.

Back when I was 24 (I am 41 now) and I went from one job to another, I had accumulated about $5,000 in Company 401k and other pretax company investments. When I left the old company, I opted to cash out my investments and take the tax hit so I could have the money in my possession. I took home about $3,800 after taxes and penalties, which was subject to another tax at the end of the year. I believe I spent the money in less than two weeks on things I cannot account for today. Had I rolled that money over into another investment vehicle like an interest-bearing annuity, I would have been better off. Here is the illustration using the future value of money theory. In 1990, $5,000 invested in an interest-bearing annuity at a periodic interest rate of 7% would have an estimated worth of $15,794.08 today. Had I known then what I know now, I could have tripled my money. The sadder part to that story is that I changed jobs and cashed in employee options one other time as well, but I will not disclose the amount because I am too embarrassed and sad to see what it would have been worth today.

Financial opportunity #3

Know the difference between depreciating and appreciating assets. This is another concept you should grasp early in life. Depreciating assets are those assets that have a greater value today than they will have tomorrow, like a car. Appreciating assets are those assets that will more than likely have a greater value in the future than they do today, like a house (in most cases and markets). The lesson here is to obtain appreciating assets and minimize or be strategic about obtaining depreciating assets. In other words, get rid of them before they cost you in terms of value.

Financial opportunity #4

Finally, make a realistic budget and stick to it! This is a harder rule to follow than any of the others, but the key here is discipline while being realistic. If it is not in the budget and not an emergency, then it does not happen. Period. End of story. I cannot tell you the number of times I have bought items or gone places based on wants and not needs and subsequently paid the price. Learn this while you are young and before you start a family. Lack of a realistic budget destroys lives and causes financial ruin, and the only one to blame for it is yourself (in my opinion)!

I would like to thank my mom for teaching me the lesson about opportunities and acting on them while the "window is open" versus waiting for the window to shut and ending up on the outside looking in!

NOTES

CHAPTER 6

Nonnegotiables

There are three times in my life that I established and reestablished what I call my nonnegotiables concerning my finances and credit. Now, you may be asking yourself, what are nonnegotiables and why is this a chapter subject? It is really quite simple. First, let me explain what I mean by nonnegotiables. Nonnegotiables are the character traits that have been instilled in me by my parents and life's experiences and are not for sale under any circumstances. These character traits are the key to my existence and the well-being of my immediate family. So there you have it, my nonnegotiables — what I would like to think is the foundation of my life!

The first time

As you now know, I am the product of both a college and a military education. During my matriculation of college and Officer Candidate School, there were several instances where I was faced with financial struggles. These struggles came about as a result of being young, inexperienced and stubborn. I can see clearly now why I had these experiences, but back then it wasn't that easy. The following is a synopsis of what I went through as a young adult attending college and Officer Candidate School for the U.S. Army.

Anyone who has completed college will tell you that it is one of the best experiences in life. While in college, I spent my entire time there hoping and praying for the day

I would graduate. After I graduated, I spent a lot of time wishing I was back in college because of all the fun I had and the lack of responsibilities at the time. All I had to do was manage to stay off academic probation and learn how to effectively manage my time, which is another way of saying have as much fun as possible while not getting in trouble with the law or campus security. I did forget to mention one thing: I also had to make sure I could pay tuition, room, board and rent. The summer before I entered college, I thought that all would be smooth sailing. Here is why I came to that conclusion.

The summer prior to my entering college, I decided to enlist (at the insistence of my father) in the U.S. Army Reserve. I did this for two reasons: I wanted to have something to do over the summer, and I wanted an additional source of income to help meet my financial needs. Now my parents did all they could to make sure I was financially prepared to go to college, and I thank them for making it possible. I attended college every semester until completion because of their efforts. Even though they did all they could, I still found it necessary to get and maintain a part-time job that would not interfere with my partying, I mean, my college studies. So after my freshman year, I vowed never to be unemployed, and to this day I have kept my word.

Upon the start of my sophomore year, I embarked on a mission to find a part-time job. I filled out every employment application I ran across, from furniture delivery, to jobs with assisted living facilities, to shoe sales. The good news is I got part-time employment as a furniture deliveryman, an assisted facility clerk and a shoe salesman. The bad news is I got fired or quit all of those jobs at one time or another due to my commitment to partying, I mean, my college studies. While employed in these positions in college, I learned many valuable lessons and had to do everything from heavy lifting, to bathing the elderly and disabled, to scrubbing bathroom floors. All of these tasks taught me two things: I did not want to make a career out of doing manual labor, and there is honor and dignity in manual labor.

Earlier in this chapter, I told you that I enlisted into the Army Reserve. While in college, I thought it would be a good idea to join the Reserved Officers Training Corps (ROTC) program as well, in hopes of getting an ROTC scholarship to help defray the cost of college. I did this also at the insistence of my father, since he would always say that if you are going to be a black man in the military, you may as well be an officer. Now, to become an officer in the military, you had to take one of three paths:

1. Reserved Officers Training Corps (ROTC)
2. Officer Candidate School (OCS)
3. Direct Commission (for skilled or specialty professions, such as an attorney or doctor)

Now of the three options, ROTC was the easiest, and since I was already enlisted in the Army Reserve (I had completed both basic training and advanced individual training), I was allowed to skip the first two years of the four-year ROTC program and go straight into the third year. This being the case, it was easy to choose ROTC over the other two options. So here I was as a first semester freshman in my third year of ROTC. Now all I had to do was apply for the scholarship the ROTC program offered, and I would be well on my way. To make a long story short, I applied for the scholarship but I did not qualify. I did not know the scholarship is awarded primarily to the person with the highest grade point average (GPA), and since I was in my first semester, I was basically ineligible. By the time I had established a valid GPA, in my second year, it still was not good enough to win outright. They had some silly rule that you had to have a 2.5 GPA or better, and I had a solid 2.0 on a 4.0 scale, which kept me out of the running. That 2.0 GPA is the same cumulative GPA I graduated with, which told me that hard work would be my lifelong friend unless I learned to work smart!

Speaking of hard work, I dropped out of the ROTC program and opted to complete my commission as a military officer by attending Officer Candidate School. This was a much tougher and grueling process, but it taught me how to overcome obstacles, instilled discipline in me and showed me how a positive attitude can defeat a negative situation. The college experience, along with the process of becoming an officer in the U.S. Army (the ROTC/OCS experience), made me a better person. This brings me to the establishment of my first nonnegotiable. There is dignity and honor in manual labor. Add to that, discipline and a positive attitude will allow you to overcome the most dismal of situations. I did not know it at the time, but these two principles became nonnegotiable for me early in my adulthood.

Reestablishment

The time or life event that caused me to reevaluate or reestablish my nonnegotiables was when I got married. This is because I had to change almost every aspect of my life. I could no longer afford to be selfish, stubborn and inflexible. Now I was taking on a wife. Any wise man that takes on a wife will acknowledge that if he is to be successful as a husband, then he must learn to put his *wants* on hold until he fulfills the *needs* of the marriage. The institution of marriage is a sacred establishment, but that establishment is truly a labor of commitment, communication and submission. Here is why I had to reestablish my nonnegotiables and add a couple!

I am married to a lovely woman who, coincidentally, has eight sisters. That's right. My wife has eight sisters, which means eight sisters-in-law and eight more reasons to love the fact that we get to visit them in St. Louis rather than live there amongst them. I say that jokingly, because I do love all of them dearly, but I also love the fact that we do not live in the same state, although they are welcome to visit at any time (just call first!). My wife is the youngest of the nine girls. Thus, all of her sisters had a hand in raising her, as only sisters can. I must say that I got the best of the bunch even though they are all beautiful women each bestowed with different blessings. The only complaint I will ever have is that when they all get together, they make more noise than a herd of cattle because they all talk to each other at the same time and in the same conversation. It is the funniest thing because they understand each other in all of the noise and confusion, but no one outside of the sisterhood can. When we all get together, the husbands immediately go to a room far, far away so we can rest our ears.

I love my wife dearly, but in accepting her as my wife, I also had to accept the teachings of her sisters. I had to accept the experiences that they poured into her as well as their teachings on how to be a woman. I must say that they did an excellent job, and I will forever be grateful for the lady they produced.

I stated at the beginning of this section that for a man marriage is about putting his wants on hold in order to fulfill the marriage's needs. The needs of a marriage that a man should fulfill are as follows:

1. To be a provider
2. To be a protector

3.   To be the leader of the house

This brings me to the reestablishment of my nonnegotiables. Along with dignity, honor, discipline and a positive attitude, I had to add being a provider, protector and leader. These were my new nonnegotiables because I was living for someone else and I had vowed not to fail her. Now, sometimes I had to remind myself of my reestablished nonnegotiables, but constant self-evaluation is a good thing.

The most recent reestablishment

On April 15, 2003, our son was born. This is the most significant event in my life next to my marriage! Our son is a gift, even though there are times that he challenges our parenting skills. Every day he reminds me through something he says or does how blessed we are to have him. Anyway, I digress. The last time I had to reestablish my goals was when he was born. I had to do so because, at the time, I had been activated for Operation Enduring Freedom as an officer in the Armed Forces. I had 19 years in the military and had planned on retiring with 20, at the ripe old age of 37. I was called up for active duty three months prior to his birth, and the possibility of not witnessing his birth or being in his life at all had crossed my mind because war was imminent.

With these thoughts weighing heavy on my mind, I did my best to be strong and shield my wife from the paranoid thoughts of the worst that could happen to me in the military during a time of war. I am sure my thoughts were no different than anyone else faced with the same dilemma today. All I could think about was, who would take care of my family if I was gone? I had life insurance and a contingency plan, but that would not take the place of my being there.

Fortunately, by the grace of God, my unit was told there was no mission for us in Iraq, since we were a combat arms unit. This was a nice way of saying it would be very expensive to send us over to Iraq and have us sit doing nothing with all those weapons and equipment built for destroying. My unit was an artillery unit and all of our equipment was expensive and required daily maintenance.

The day I informed my wife of the change and that I would be home to witness the birth of our son was one of the happiest days of my life. It is also the day I realized I had to get serious about my goals. This brings me to the last time I evaluated and reestablished my nonnegotiables. They now are: to act with dignity, honor, discipline, and a positive attitude, to be protector, provider, leader, father and a role model and, finally, to have strong faith. These are the traits I must possess and they are not negotiable for the duration of my existence on this earth. Now you may ask how these nonnegotiables relate to the title of the book. I will attempt to provide a simple explanation:

- I must carry myself with dignity at all times.
- I will act honorably.
- Discipline will guide my actions.
- A positive attitude will determine my attitude.
- I will protect my family at all times.
- I will provide for my family.
- I am the head of my household, but it is alright to let my wife take the lead from time to time on certain issues.
- Being a father is a 24-hour-a-day seven-days-a-week job.

- I take the job of role model seriously, as a husband, father, brother and friend.
- Strong faith will guide me when nothing else will.

All of these nonnegotiables will make me a wealthy man. I want to be wealthy with love, family and faith. Common sense teaches me that wealth is not your material possessions but rather that which cannot be taken away.

NOTES

CHAPTER 7

Second-guessing Yourself

How many times have you been faced with a situation concerning your finances, and you were hesitant about what to do next? How many times have you been faced with a decision, and you made a decision but were unsure and changed your mind? How many times have you been faced with a financial dilemma, made a decision but in the back of your mind wanted to go in a different direction; then, after the event and its results, you discover you could have profited had you not changed your mind. The culprit in all of these scenarios is you. Yes, you are your own worst enemy, and you are so because you have made the mistake of second-guessing yourself. In this chapter, I would like to address second-guessing and why it happens. I would also like to give you several strategies that may work for you if you do not second-guess yourself.

Who are you really second-guessing?

We have all been there. We have all had to make a decision about something and then, after some thought, have second-guessed that decision and changed our mind. After we have changed our mind, the results come in about the decision we made and we find that had we stuck to the initial decision, we would have benefited. How many times has that happened to you? I can tell you that it has happened to me several times and has cost me each time. If I could go back in time and relive those situations, knowing what I know now, I would have stuck to my initial decision. Since we know we cannot travel back in time, I can only share with you the life lesson I have learned from second-guessing myself.

When you are second-guessing yourself, you are really second-guessing the universe, or what I know as a higher power. That higher power created the heavens and earth and all that exists on it. When you second-guess yourself, you are second-guessing your sound judgment and your moral thoughts. You are second-guessing what life has taught you, and you are impacting your future. Sometimes you impact your future in a negative way and sometimes in a positive way. In any event, you lose when you second-guess yourself, so please take ownership of your decisions.

When making a decision, be sure the decision is well thought out before you proceed and seek counsel, if needed, before you act. Once you have done that, you will find your first instinct is the right one, especially when it comes to your finances. You may not always like the decision, but in time you will see that if your decision is guided by a higher power, it will always work out in your favor.

Strategy #1 (buying a home at the age of 21)

In the United States, people are considered adults at the age of 21. Another term for this is *legal*. You are no longer considered a minor and are afforded all of the rights and privileges of an adult that is 100 years old. You have the right to do anything allowed by law. This being the case, why not become a homeowner? Is this a crazy idea? At the early age of 21, most adults are not considered responsible enough to handle a mortgage. Most 21-year-olds are either in college or just entering the workforce, and they do not know what the future holds for them. Consider this: homeowners as a group have more disposable income than non-homeowners and are more likely to generate wealth! Here are some benefits of owning a home early in adulthood.

<u>Solid credit foundation.</u> Since this is probably the largest single purchase you will make in your life, your credit will be heavily scrutinized, and you will be deemed creditworthy if you are approved by a lender to purchase a home.

<u>Better credit, better choices.</u> Since, as a homeowner, your credit is better because, you will be forced to make better choices concerning your finances, thus putting yourself in a better financial situation.

<u>Ownership versus renting.</u> Being a homeowner will afford you certain tax benefits non-homeowners cannot take advantage of.

<u>Increased income.</u> Since you are a homeowner at such a young age, you can have a roommate and charge him/her rent as your income.

<u>Pride of ownership.</u> Owning a home gives you a certain pride of ownership that will carry over into your professional life and cause you to work smarter, thus accomplishing more.

Strategy #2 (forming an investment club)

An investment club is a group of individuals who pool their monies for the purpose of making sound investments. The ultimate goal of an investment club is to generate a profit. This is done by making investment purchases based on an analysis of the investment vehicles that have shown good performance and a sound track record. The way an investment club works is a testament to why young adults should look into forming one. An investment club helps drive the entrepeurial spirit.

Generate income

The number one goal of most young adults is to make money. What better way do you know of making money than investing in the stock market? Outside of hitting the lottery, this is a safe bet with more benefits than just making money.

Become better informed

The way the profitable investment clubs work is their members do ample research on their investment selections prior to making a decision as to whether to invest or not. In doing this research, the individuals become better informed about the issues surrounding the investment as well as about ancillary products. Quite often, this process forces you to patronize the very products you invest in.

Gain financial maturity

What better way to gain financial awareness than to form an investment club at an early age with a group of your peers. You can agree to select stocks for products that you all use and learn more about the companies that produce them.

Develop financial discipline

The financial discipline gained from properly engaging in this process will have lifelong benefits.

Strategy #3 (start a long-term annuity at the age of 21)

This strategy is so simple to grasp that I will not use that many words to explain it. Rather I will use numbers and the future value theory.

If you invest $100 monthly at an annual interest rate of 7% it will be worth

- $28,955 by the time you are 35

- $74,699 by the time you are 45

- $164,684 by the time you are 55

- $341,699 by the time you are 65

If you invest a one-time lump sum of $5,000 at an annual interest rate of 7% it will be worth

- $12,892.67 by the time you are 35
- $25,361.83 by the time you are 45
- $49,890.57 by the time you are 55
- $98,142.30 by the time you are 65

Given the previous illustrations, is this not a simple concept to grasp? Are either of the two examples attainable for most 21-year-olds? I hope the answers to these two questions are both yes. If not, then maybe you should consider this strategy regardless of your age, because we all know someone who could benefit from having more money. One of these strategies could work for you.

The last point I want to make about these illustrations is that you do not have to be a rocket scientist in order to save money. It just takes time to figure out the strategy that works for you.

Strategy #4 (never buy a new car)

The first thing I did when I graduated from college was to buy a new car. It was a silver 1990 Nissan Pulsar, and it was loaded. But in retrospect I would have been better served by buying a quality used car or getting my old hooptie repaired. Here is why I say never buy a new car:

Most cars are a depreciating asset

That's right. Cars, for the most part, are a depreciating asset. By this I mean, as soon as you drive the car off of the lot, it loses value. Estimates show that the average car loses approximately $1,000 of its book value the minute it is purchased and driven home. Now, unless your new car will last you seven to ten years, you never really get your money's worth out of the purchase. Instead, you end up buying another new car and starting the process all over again. Some alternatives to buying a new car are

- using public transportation
- investing in a bicycle
- purchasing a certified pre-owned vehicle

Strategy #5 (make your good credit work for you)

Credit scores range from a low of 350 to a high of 850. Anyone that has faced some credit challenges will tell you that once you overcome those challenges, you will do everything in your power to never go down that path again.

Here are some management tips that may work for you

- Pay your bills on time.
- Negotiate interest rates on credit cards whenever possible.
- Keep your credit card balances at 40% or less of the established limit.
- Review a copy of your credit reports at least once a year.

- Know that there are only three credit reporting agencies in the United States, and they are Equifax, TransUnion and Experian.

- Know and understand how the FICO scoring system works.

- Use your credit cards for travel and/or emergencies only.

- You only need one major credit card (Visa, MasterCard, Discover or American Express)

- Never cosign for credit with someone else.

- Know the home ownership process before you start the process.

- Learn the mortgage terminology (lingo).

- Understand the different mortgage products that are out there.

- Learn how to negotiate effectively with your creditors.

- Guard against identity theft.

- Never buy credit life insurance.

- Know that the wealth-building process often starts with home ownership.

NOTES

CHAPTER 8

Wall Street vs. Your Street

How often do you turn on the news or open the newspaper and find that the subject of the article or clip is Wall Street? Do you ever wonder how the activities of Wall Street impact what is occurring on your street? What makes stock prices go up? What makes stock prices go down? Should you invest in the stock market? In this chapter, I will attempt to provide a better understanding of the stock market and what role it plays in our economy!

The Stock Market
Definition

The expression "stock market" refers to the system that enables the trading of company stocks (collective shares), other securities, and derivatives. Bonds are still traditionally traded in an informal, over the counter market known as the bond market. Commodities are traded in what is called the "commodities markets," and derivatives are traded in a variety of markets (but, like bonds, mostly "over-the-counter").

The size of the worldwide "bond market" is estimated at $45 trillion. The size of the "stock market" is estimated at about $51 trillion. The world derivatives market has been estimated at about $480 trillion "face" or nominal value, 30 times the size of the U.S. economy ... and 12 times the size of the entire world economy. The stocks are listed and traded on the stock exchange which are entities (a corporation or mutual organization) specialized in the business of bringing buyers and sellers of stocks and securities together. The stock market in the United States includes the trading of all securities listed on the New York Stock Exchange (NYSE), the NASDAQ, the Amex, as well as on the many regional exchanges. European examples of stock exchanges include the Paris Bourse (now part of Euronext), the London Stock Exchange and the Deutsche Börse.

Trading

Participants in the stock market range from small individual stock investors to large hedge fund traders, who can be based anywhere. Their orders usually end up with a professional at a stock exchange, who executes the order.

Some exchanges are physical locations where transactions are carried out on a trading floor, by a method known as open outcry. This type of auction is used in stock exchanges and commodity exchanges where traders may enter "verbal" bids and offers simultaneously. The other type of exchange is a virtual kind, composed of a network of computers where trades are made electronically via traders.

Actual trades are based on an auction market paradigm where a potential buyer bids a specific price for a stock and a potential seller asks a specific price for the stock. (Buying or selling *at market* means you will accept *any* ask price or bid price for the stock, respectively.) When the bid and ask prices match, a sale takes place on a first come first served basis if there are multiple bidders or askers at a given price.

The purpose of a stock exchange is to facilitate the exchange of securities between buyers and sellers, thus providing a marketplace (virtual or real). The exchanges provide real-time trading information on the listed securities, facilitating price discovery.

The New York Stock Exchange is a physical exchange, also referred to as a listed exchange — only stocks listed with the exchange may be traded. Orders enter by way of exchange members and flow down to a specialist, who goes to the floor trading post to trade stock. The specialist's job is to match buy and sell orders using open outcry.

If a spread exists, no trade immediately takes place — in this case the specialist should use his/her own resources (money or stock) to close the difference after his/her judged time. Once a trade has been made the details are reported on the "tape" and sent back to the brokerage firm, which then notifies the investor who placed the order. Although there is a significant amount of human contact in this process, computers play an important role, especially for so-called "program trading".

The NASDAQ is a virtual listed exchange, where all of the trading is done over a computer network. The process is similar to the New York Stock Exchange. However, buyers and sellers are electronically matched. One or more NASDAQ market makers will always provide a bid and ask price at which they will always purchase or sell "their" stock.

From time to time, active trading (especially in large blocks of securities) have moved away from the "active" exchanges. Securities firms, led by UBS AG, Goldman Sachs Group Inc. and Credit Suisse Group, already steer 12 percent of U.S. security trades away from the exchanges to their internal systems. That share probably will increase to 18 percent by 2010 as more investment banks bypass the NYSE and NASDAQ and pair buyers and sellers of securities themselves, according to data compiled by Boston-based Aite Group LLC, a brokerage-industry consultant.

Now that computers have eliminated the need for trading floors like the Big Board's, the balance of power in equity markets is shifting. By bringing more orders in-house, where clients can move big blocks of stock *anonymously*, brokers pay the exchanges less in fees and capture a bigger share of the $11 billion a year that institutional investors pay in trading commissions.

Market participants

Many years ago, worldwide, buyers and sellers were individual investors, such as wealthy businessmen, with long family histories (and emotional ties) to particular corporations. Over time, markets have become more "institutionalized"; buyers and sellers are largely institutions (e.g., pension funds, insurance companies, mutual funds, hedge funds, investor groups, and banks). The rise of the institutional investor has brought with it some improvements in market operations. Thus, the government was responsible for "fixed" (and exorbitant) fees being markedly reduced for the "small" investor, but only after the large institutions had managed to break the brokers' solid front on fees (they then went to "negotiated" fees, but only for large institutions).

However, corporate governance (at least in the West) has been very much adversely affected by the rise of (largely "absentee") institutional "owners."

History

Historian Fernand Braudel suggests that in Cairo in the 11th century Muslim and Jewish merchants had already set up every form of trade association and had knowledge of every method of credit and payment, disproving the belief that these were invented later by Italians. In 12th century France, the *courratiers de change* were concerned with managing and regulating the debts of agricultural communities on behalf of the banks. Because these men also traded with debts, they could be called the first brokers. In late 13th century Bruges commodity traders gathered inside the house of a man called *Van der Beurse*, and in 1309 they became the "Brugse Beurse," institutionalizing what had been, until then, an informal meeting. The idea quickly spread around Flanders and neighboring counties and "Beurzen" soon opened in Ghent and Amsterdam.

In the middle of the 13th century Venetian bankers began to trade in government securities. In 1351 the Venetian government outlawed spreading rumors intended to lower the price of government funds. Bankers in Pisa, Verona, Genoa and Florence also began trading in government securities during the 14th century. This was only possible because these were independent city states not ruled by a duke but a council of influential citizens. The Dutch later started joint stock companies, which let shareholders invest in business ventures and get a share of their profits — or losses. In 1602, the Dutch East India Company issued the first shares on the Amsterdam Stock Exchange. It was the first company to issue stocks and bonds.

The Amsterdam Stock Exchange is also said to have been the first stock exchange to introduce continuous trade in the early 17th century. The Dutch "pioneered short selling, option trading, debt-equity swaps, merchant banking, unit trusts and other speculative instruments, much as we know them" (Murray Sayle, "Japan Goes Dutch," *London Review of Books* XXIII. 7, April 5, 2001). There are now stock markets in virtually every developed and most developing economies, with the world's biggest markets being in the United States, Canada, China (Hong Kong), India, UK, Germany, France and Japan.

The importance of the stock market

The stock market is one of the most important sources for companies to raise money. This allows businesses to go public, or raise additional capital for expansion. The liquidity that an exchange provides affords investors the ability to quickly and easily sell securities. This is an attractive feature of investing in stocks, compared to other less liquid investments such as real estate.

History has shown that the price of shares and other assets is an important part of the dynamics of economic activity, and can influence or be an indicator of social mood. Rising share prices, for instance, tend to be associated with increased business investment and vice versa. Share prices also affect the wealth of households and their consumption. Therefore, central banks tend to keep an eye on the control and behavior of the stock market and, in general, on the smooth operation of financial system functions.

Exchanges also act as the clearinghouse for each transaction, meaning that they collect and deliver the shares, and guarantee payment to the seller of a security. This eliminates the risk to an individual buyer or seller that the counter party could default on the transaction.

The smooth functioning of all these activities facilitates economic growth in that lower costs and enterprise risks promote the production of goods and services as well as employment. In this way the financial system contributes to increased prosperity.

Relation of the stock market to the modern financial system

The financial system in most western countries has undergone a remarkable transformation. One feature of this development is disintermediation. A portion of the funds involved in saving and financing flows directly to the financial markets instead of being routed via banks' traditional lending and deposit operations. The general public's heightened interest in investing in the stock market, either directly or through mutual funds, has been an important component of this process. Statistics show that in recent decades shares have made up an increasingly large proportion of households' financial assets in many countries. In the 1970s, in Sweden, deposit accounts and other very liquid assets with little risk made up almost 60 per cent of households' financial wealth, compared to less than 20 per cent in the 2000s.

The major part of this adjustment in financial portfolios has gone directly to shares but a good deal now takes the form of various kinds of institutional investment for groups of individuals, e.g., pension funds, mutual funds, hedge funds, insurance investment of premiums, etc. The trend towards forms of saving with a higher risk has been accentuated by new rules for most funds and insurance, permitting a higher proportion of shares to bonds. Similar tendencies are to be found in other industrialized countries. In all developed economic systems, such as the European Union, the United States, Japan and other developed nations, the trend has been the same: saving has moved away from traditional (government insured) bank deposits to more risky securities of one sort or another.

The stock market, individual investors, and financial risk

Riskier long-term saving requires that an *individual* possess the ability to manage the associated increased risks. Stock prices fluctuate widely, in marked contrast to the stability of (government insured) bank deposits or bonds. This is something that could affect not only the individual investor or household, but also the economy on a large scale. The following deals with some of the risks of the financial sector in general and the stock market in particular. This is certainly more important now that so many newcomers have entered the stock market, or have acquired other "risky" investments (such as "investment" property, i.e., real estate and collectables).

The behavior of the stock market

From experience we know that investors may temporarily pull financial prices away from their long term trend level. Over-reactions may occur — so that excessive optimism (euphoria) may drive prices unduly high or excessive pessimism may drive prices unduly low. New theoretical and empirical arguments have been put forward against the notion that financial markets are efficient.

According to some experts in the business, only changes in fundamental factors, such as profits or dividends, ought to affect share prices. The stock market crash in 1987 proved this theory to be incorrect when the Dow Jones index plummeted 22.6 percent which was the largest one day fall in the United States. This event demonstrated that share prices can fall dramatically even though, to this day, it is impossible to fix a definite cause to account for the crash.

Various explanations for large price movements have been proclaimed. For instance, some research has shown that changes in estimated risk, and the use of certain strategies, such as stop-loss limits and Value at Risk limits, theoretically could cause financial markets to overreact.

Other research has shown that psychological factors may result in exaggerated stock price movements. Psychological research has demonstrated that people are predisposed to "seeing" patterns, and often will perceive a pattern in what is, in fact, just noise. In the present context this means that a succession of good news items about a company may lead investors to overreact positively (unjustifiably driving the price up). A period of good returns also boosts the investor's self-confidence, reducing his (psychological) risk threshold.

Another phenomenon (also from psychology) that works against an objective assessment is "group thinking." As social animals, it is not easy to stick to an opinion that differs markedly from that of a majority of the group. An example with which one may be familiar is the reluctance to enter a restaurant that is empty; people generally prefer to have their opinion validated by those of others in the group.

Another example is to draw an analogy with gambling. In normal times the market behaves like a game of roulette; the probabilities are known and largely independent of the investment decisions of the different players. In times of market stress, however, the game becomes more like poker (herding behavior takes over). The players now must give heavy weight to the psychology of other investors and how they are likely to react psychologically.

The stock market, as any other business, is quite unforgiving of amateurs. Inexperienced investors rarely get the assistance and support they need. In the period running up to the recent NASDAQ crash, less than 1 per cent of the analysts' recommendations had been to sell (and even during the 2000–2002 crash, the average did not rise above 5%). The media amplified the general euphoria, with reports of rapidly rising share prices and the notion that large sums of money could be quickly earned in the so-called new economy stock market.

Irrational behavior

Sometimes the market tends to react irrationally to economic news, even if that news has no real affect on the technical value of securities itself. Therefore, the stock market can be swayed tremendously in either direction by press releases, rumors and mass panic.

Over the short-term, stocks and other securities can be battered or buoyed by any number of fast market-changing events, making the stock market difficult to predict.

Stock market index

The movements of the prices in a market or section of a market are captured in price indices called stock market indices, of which there are many, e.g., the S&P, the FTSE and the Euronext indices. Such indices are usually market capitalization (the total market value of floating capital of the company) weighted, with the weights reflecting the contribution of the stock to the index.

Derivative instruments

Financial innovation has brought many new financial instruments whose pay-offs or values depend on the prices of stocks. Some examples are exchange-traded funds (ETFs), stock index and stock options, equity swaps, single-stock futures, and stock index futures. These last two may be traded on futures exchanges (which are distinct from stock exchanges and their history traces back to commodities futures exchanges), or traded over-the-counter. As all of these products are only *derived* from stocks, they are sometimes considered to be traded in a (hypothetical) derivatives market, rather than the (hypothetical) stock market.

Leveraged Strategies

Stocks that a trader does not actually own may be traded using short selling; margin buying may be used to purchase stock with borrowed funds; or, *derivatives* may be used to control large blocks of stocks for a much smaller amount of money than would be required by outright purchase or sale.

Short selling

In short selling, the trader borrows stock (usually from his brokerage which holds its clients' shares or its own shares on account to lend to short sellers) then sells it on the market, hoping for the price to fall. The trader eventually buys back the stock, making money if the price fell in the meantime or losing money if it rose. Exiting a short position by buying back the stock is called "covering a short position." This strategy may also be used by unscrupulous traders to artificially lower the price of a stock. Hence most markets either prevent short selling or place restrictions on when and how a short sale can occur. The practice of naked shorting is illegal in most (but not all) stock markets.

Margin buying

In margin buying, the trader borrows money (at interest) to buy a stock and hopes for it to rise. Most industrialized countries have regulations that require that if the borrowing is based on collateral from other stocks the trader owns outright, it can be a maximum of a certain percentage of those other stocks' value. In the United States, the margin requirements have been 50% for many years (that is, if you want to make a $1000 investment, you need to put up $500, and there is often a maintenance margin below the $500). A margin call is made if the total value of the investor's account cannot support the loss of the trade. (Upon a decline in the value of the margined securities additional funds may be required to maintain the account's equity, and with or without notice the margined security or any others within the account may be sold by the brokerage to protect its loan position. The investor is responsible for any shortfall following such forced sales.) Regulation of margin requirements (by the Federal Reserve) was implemented after the Crash of 1929. Before that, speculators typically only needed to put up as little as 10 percent (or even less) of the total investment represented by the stocks purchased. Other rules may include the prohibition of *free-riding:* putting in an order to buy stocks without paying initially (there is normally a three-day grace period for delivery of the stock), but then selling them (before the three-days are up) and using part of the proceeds to make the original payment (assuming that the value of the stocks has not declined in the interim).

Investment strategies

One of the many things people always want to know about the stock market is, "How do I make money investing?" There are many different approaches; two basic methods are classified as either fundamental analysis or technical analysis. Fundamental analysis refers to analyzing companies by their financial statements found in SEC Filings, business trends, general economic conditions, etc. Technical analysis studies price actions in markets through the use of charts and quantitative techniques to attempt to forecast price trends regardless of the company's financial prospects.

Additionally, many choose to invest via the index method. In this method, one holds a weighted or unweighted portfolio consisting of the entire stock market or some segment of the stock market (such as the S&P 500). The principal aim of this strategy is to maximize diversification, minimize taxes from too frequent trading, and ride the general trend of the stock market (which, in the U.S., has averaged nearly 10% per year, compounded annually, since World War II).

Source: Wikipedia, "The Stock Market"

With all of that being said, I will end this chapter by answering the questions in a sweet and concise manner or, as my father would say, "don't use twenty words when two will do"!

How do the activities of Wall Street impact what is occurring on your street? The short answer is the opposite is true — what happens on your street impacts the activities of Wall Street!

What makes stock prices fluctuate up? Rumors, analyst predictions, comments from government officials, the feds, industry trends etc.!

Should you invest in the stock market? Yes. Historically, it is one of the most secure ways to make money once you have a complete understanding of what you are doing!

There you have it! My explanation of the stock market (with help from "Wikipedia") and my views from a common sense perspective on what the stock market is, what makes stock prices fluctuate and my answer to whether you should invest via the stock market!

NOTES

CHAPTER 9

People (show you who and what they are)

Some of the best advice I have ever gotten was this: "People, regardless of what stage of life they are in, will show you who and what they are." Since life has reinforced this profound statement to me over and over again, I have no choice but to accept it. This being the case, I have a revised version of the statement, and it goes a little something like this: "Once people show you who and what they are, believe them." The reason I revised the statement is so it can be applied to all people. No matter whom the person is — their education, experience, financial status or physical looks — they are who they show you they are by how they respond to adversity.

In my 41 years, I have encountered all types of people in the financial industry. They have all taught me something by showing me who and what they are. The classifications of people I will discuss have characteristics I compare to animals. Please do not take offense when I make these comparisons because this is my book. If you disagree, then write your own book. These are the people I have encountered in the financial industry and the lessons they taught me!

Predators

By definition, a predator is an organism that exists by preying on other organisms. My interpretation of this, concerning people, is the same. There are people in this world that make their living by preying on the misfortunes of other people. This is especially true in the financial industry. Believe it or not, there are companies that extend credit and lend money or other goods and services that promote and reward the predator mentality. These companies recruit and grow individuals and teach them to become predators. What does a predator look like? You may ask. How can I recognize a predator?

How can I avoid being preyed on?

Recognizing a predator is not as easy as one may think! They are usually people that look and act just like you. The only difference is their agenda. A predator preys on the underserved, under informed and, for lack of a better word, the ignorant. Predators smell you coming from a mile away; they look for "buzz" words in your conversation. They ask leading questions, awaiting a certain response. They are usually great salesmen. They are often very personable and display great attitudes to lure you into the trap. Once you are trapped, they go for the kill!

Watch out for predators in your dealings with:

- Finance companies
- Car dealerships
- Mortgage companies and brokers
- Attorneys
- Insurance salesmen
- Contractors

The list goes on and on!

Now, you may be asking yourself, since predators are every where, how can I recognize them and avoid them? My response to that is you usually do not recognize predators until you are right in front of them and there is no way to avoid them. You have to stand your ground. The way you stand your ground is by asking questions. Ask enough questions to make an informed decision about the matter. If you are buying a house and dealing with someone in the mortgage industry, ask for the interest rate and the APR (annual percentage rate). Ask what the fees are that make up the closing costs and prepaid items. If you are applying for a credit card, ask for the lowest interest rate. Ask about the terms of the repayment policy. If you are looking to finance a car, ask how the dealership's financing compares to a credit union's financing. You see, the more questions you ask a predator, the more you are likely to get answers that allow you to make an informed decision. This also shows the predator that while they may be dealing with someone inexperienced, they are also dealing with someone that will not be taken advantage of! Predators look for the weak individuals or those that appear to be victims. Don't be a victim, and don't let others prey on you!

How can you avoid being preyed on? In addition to asking questions in order to make informed decisions, you should do your level best to educate yourself prior to making any purchases or making any inquiries concerning your credit. It is always good to ask others that know more than you do about a certain issue. I think it is infinitely better to do the research *yourself* on the issue. This way you can form your own opinion instead of that of someone else. If you can evaluate the facts based on your own understanding, then that gives you confidence. That confidence manifests itself when you are making the purchase, closing the loan or accepting the terms of the credit card. That confidence also gets you a better deal and keeps you from being preyed on, and thus, you are not the victim.

Vultures

Vultures are rather large birds that feed on other animals after they have expired. There are people that act like vultures as well. As an example, I present to you the family that is behind on their debts and facing the possibility of losing their home through foreclosure. For argument's sake, let's say there is no way they can catch up on their bills, and they are faced with losing their home if they do not catch up the mortgage note in 60 days. Because of the type of mortgage they entered into, they have a term that has taken their payments from $750 per month to $1,050 per month. They entered into this type of mortgage because they were told by the broker that it was all they qualified for based on their income and credit. They trusted him and closed on the home, and three years later this is the situation they are faced with. In other words, they were preyed upon.

Now, along comes this guy offering to save the day by buying the house from the owners and renting it back to them at a term that allows them to save money plus catch up on their other debts. This being the case, they take the deal. They end up losing the home anyway because the buyer evicts them and ends up selling the home for a profit. This is an example of what vultures do. They take advantage of those that have already been victimized. You can avoid vultures the same way you avoid predators, and that is through educating yourself about the facts and possible outcomes of your situation.

Turkeys

My dad once told me that turkeys have to be shielded from the rain. I asked him why. He said that when it rains, turkeys look up to see where the rain is coming from. In doing so, the rain goes down their noses and they drown. I asked him why again. He said because no one made them come in from the rain. I am reminded of this story often, whenever I see people that do not use good judgment when making a financial transaction and it has a negative effect on them or their circumstances. You see, an adult turkey has encountered rain and has learned to avoid it because of the consequences. Some people are just like turkeys that drown when it rains. They know that the outcome of the choice they are about to make will lead to something negative; however, they proceed with the decision. Afterwards, they ask themselves why they did not exercise better judgment.

People that act like turkeys need someone else to do their thinking for them because if they did it for themselves, they would drown. My point here is we should all try to avoid turkeys. In your life, you will meet someone who needs to be told to come in from the rain. Do your best to help them, but if they do not listen, leave them be!

Eagles

We all know what eagles are. In our culture, the eagle is the most majestic of birds. We often say phrases like "fly high like an eagle" or "soar high like an eagle." The same is true with people. In my estimation the people I have encountered that are eagles are those that find a way to succeed no matter what the odds. These are the people that wake up in the morning with the goal of achievement as their motto. No matter the situation, eagles find a way to succeed by whatever ethical means possible, no matter the personal sacrifice. Eagles do not see problems, they see challenges; they don't see failure, they see an opportunity to do better the next time around; they don't see situations as win or lose, they see situations as win or learn. Eagles are the type of people others want to be around because when you are around an eagle, you can feel the positive energy and you eventually want to soar as high as they do.

In my career, I have met several eagles that still work in the financial industry. These are the people that empower you with solutions. An eagle will be faced with a challenge and will find the right solution. They display passion and commitment to what they do. Unlike the predator or vulture, they lift others up and point them in the direction they should be going. Here is one of my eagle encounters.

I once worked for a finance company where our service was the extension, management and collection of money. We would extend credit to worthy customers with the ultimate goal of financing or refinancing their mortgages and saving the customers money. One day a customer came in nervous and panicking because the pipes had burst in his house. He lived in a two-story with a basement, and the second floor had major damage. At this time, I was a trainee and I had limited to no experience in these matters. My manager, the eagle, took the customer in the conference room and offered him something to drink. My manager came out to me and said, "Let me show you how you are going to win a customer for life." We pulled the customer's credit and saw that while he had a high credit score, he was maxed out on all his credit cards and had three car notes. The eagle asked me what I thought of the credit report. I responded with, "I see a customer with a great credit score and debt," and I said I thought that there was nothing we could do for him. He asked me what else I saw. I responded with, "I see a mortgage." He said, "Yes, you see a mortgage. Now, go in there and tell the customer that we can help him." He told me to go in there and say with confidence, "Mr. Customer, I want you to go home and bring me all of your mortgage documents from when you closed on your home." I was nervous because

I was new and I did not know what I was doing, but I did just what my manager asked me to, and I did it with confidence. The customer looked at me, shook his head and proceeded to do as I asked.

When he walked out, my manager said, "Now, all you have to do is get him approved to refinance his home and consolidate all of his debt." I responded with, "I do?" He said, "Yes you do!" I responded back with, "I don't know what to do!" He said, "Neither did I when I had my first customer in that situation, but you are about to find out." To make a long story short, I completed the necessary application on behalf of the customer and got it submitted to our underwriting department, which responded with an approval. The next day, the customer came in with the requested documents and I told him what we were going to do. We were going to refinance his home while paying off all of his outstanding debt, and we were going to give him enough money to make the repairs on his home plus put $5,000 away in savings. There were two conditions: he had to agree to the terms of the refinancing, and he had to move all of his accounts over to our financial institution. He agreed, and my manager said, "That is how you win a customer for life."

As I stated earlier, eagles don't see problems; they see challenges. And challenges can be overcome!

Geese

A goose is another interesting bird and unique in a lot of ways. Did you know that geese fly from different parts of the country, traveling hundreds of miles on a seasonal basis? Did you know that when geese fly, they fly in a particular pattern? They fly in a V pattern, and they do this for efficiency. You see, the lead goose flies at the point of the V, taking the full force of the wind or turbulence. The geese that are down the line actually benefit from the geese that are in front of them because of the draft that is created, allowing them to rest a bit as they fly. When the lead goose gets tired, he falls to the back of the formation and another goose takes the lead. Now this is not a documentary on geese, but I tell this story because of what the geese do while flying. Can you guess what that is? They honk at each other. Do you know why they honk at each other? They honk at each other to encourage each other to continue on their journey. They honk at each other, specifically at the lead goose, to give him confidence and tell him he is doing a great job. This encouragement helps him fly stronger and longer than if he were flying alone. The other point I wanted to make about geese is that when a goose falls out of formation in order to land and rest, at least one other goose will fly down with him so that he does not take the remainder of the journey alone.

There are people I know that are exactly like geese! They provide encouragement when you are leading. If you fall, they do not let you fall alone. They provide support and encouragement just like geese do. Suffice it to say that after you have fallen behind and rested and are ready to return to the flying formation, they are right there to provide encouragement to help you get back in line. These are the people that lead by example, and they in turn show you how to lead.

Lions

We all know that lions are the kings of the jungle. They have this title because no other animal in the jungle will attack a lion. You are probably also aware that lions live in packs called a pride. They live in theses prides as a family, with the male lion as the head. He is the protector of the pride. He knows that the responsibility of ensuring that no harm comes to his pride and that no one takes over his territory is his alone. He understands and accepts his role and carries out his responsibility as the leader. Some people are like lions; they understand their role and take the responsibility seriously, just like a lion. They are fearless in their commitment and resolve even when it is unpopular.

If you consider the corporate world, in this case the financial corporate world, a jungle, then you will at some point encounter the person that is the lion of his pride. These are the people that see the task and take ownership. They do not pass the buck, and if they fall short of the desired results, they own up to it and do not shirk the blame. When they succeed, they share the glory!

There you have it. I have now categorized the types of people I have encountered during my career in the financial industry. You may not see the correlation and how it applies to building common sense, so let me summarize:

- Predators prey on the underserved and misinformed.
- Vultures take advantage of you after you have been victimized.
- Turkeys need to be told what to do.
- Eagles set their goals high and strive to achieve them.
- Geese offer encouragement when it is your turn to lead.
- Lions accept responsibility no matter the task.

These characterizations of the people I have encountered have helped me gain judgment and ultimately greater common sense!

NOTES

CHAPTER 10

Applying Your Common Sense

Now that I have told you a little bit of my story while trying to impart some common sense lessons I have learned, let me try to sum it all up! In this summary, I will attempt to illustrate how each of the chapters addresses common sense from a financial perspective and at the same time to pass on some knowledge you may find beneficial!

Sum Total

As I stated at the beginning of chapter 1, we are all the sum total of our life's experiences. How does this apply to common sense and help you from a financial standpoint? Your life's experiences have shaped you into the person you are. For the most part, the only thing that is going to change about you is the people with whom you associate. Take advantage of the lessons life teaches you when it comes to finances. Here are the points I hoped I conveyed in chapter 1:

- It is not a mistake if you do not repeat it.
- Use good judgment concerning your finances.
- Do not make financial decisions based on emotion; be rational.
- Be frugal in times of prosperity.
- Heed the lesson in failure.

- Always work with a budget and stick to it.
- Consider times of adversity as character-building experiences.
- Business has no friends.

Credit Grantors

I gave a very funny but true story in chapter 2 about the proposal process I went through with my wife. What I don't want to be overlooked is the main point of the story. My point in this chapter was very simple: your name is the cover to your character; your character is what people remember when you are not around. Your credit rating is a snapshot of your character and the way financial institutions and others that extend credit see you. You are in control of your character and should make sure your character reflects the following:

- Substance
- Responsibility
- Integrity
- Commitment to your obligations
- Intelligence

Credit History

As adults, we all should have some idea of how our credit history can help or hurt us. We should all know our FICO score and how the scoring system works. Finally, we should know our rights concerning our credit. Below are some highlights:

- Safeguard your identity.
- Be wary of cosigning for credit.

- Review a copy of your credit report every 6 to 12 months.

- Try to limit your credit card debt to 50% or less of the limit.

- Do not be afraid to deal with your creditors when you are delinquent.

Success Before Work

In this chapter, I talked about my father and how hard he worked. I talked about how he instilled principles in me through the work he would make me do. I also talked about how he taught me that I must be willing to do the work in order to achieve success. Here are some other points I attempted to convey:

- Be thorough.
- Get organized.
- Be meticulous.
- Apply backwards planning whenever possible.

Financial Opportunities

In this chapter, I shared one of the many lessons my mom taught me about opportunities. I talked about establishing a savings plan and gave a guideline to adhere to. When my mom reads this, she will probably be surprised to know that she taught me this. Below are some other points from this chapter:

- Pay yourself first.
- Make wise choices with your 401k as you transition from one employer to another.

- Know the difference between depreciating and appreciating assets.
- Understand the benefits of a sound budget.

Nonnegotiables

In this chapter, I talked about the times I had to establish and reestablish those things I considered nonnegotiables, and they are

- Carry yourself with dignity at all times.
- Act with honor.
- Let discipline guide your actions.
- Attitude determines altitude.
- Protect and provide for the ones you love.
- Let faith be your guide.

Second-guessing Yourself

In chapter 7, I talked about self-doubt and how it can sometimes cause difficulties in your life. I addressed who the culprit is in this scenario and why. I talked about thinking things through and using sound judgment. I also gave you some strategies to consider concerning your finances. These are listed below:

- Consider buying a home at the age of 21.
- Form an investment club.
- Gain financial maturity.
- Develop financial discipline.
- Invest your money at an early age.
- Make your credit work for you.

- Become an informed consumer.

Wall Street vs. Your Street

In this chapter, I attempted to explain, with some help from Wikipedia, how the stock market works. I hope you found it informative as most of the people I know struggle to understand it.

People (show you who and what they are)

In chapter 9, I attempted to characterize the types of people I have encountered during my career. This by no means is an account of all of the people I have met but rather a summary of the types of people that can hinder you in the finance industry or help you!

These are the ones you should avoid:

- Predators
- Vultures
- Turkeys

These are the ones you should seek out and learn from:

- Eagles
- Geese
- Lions

All of these people I have encountered in my career taught me something, and I am thankful for the lesson.

10 things all adults should know from a Common Sense perspective

1. Know your credit history and FICO score!

2. Never cosign for anyone for credit unless you are prepared to pay the debt!

3. Purchasing a certified pre-owned automobile instead of a new one makes economical sense!

4. You only need one major credit card!

5. Credit cards should be used for emergencies and travel only!

6. If you have to use a credit card for purchases, never charge anything you cannot pay off in 30 days!

7. Owning your home instead of renting your home is a winning strategy!

8. Develop an investment/savings strategy early in your adult life!

9. Do your level best to negotiate your rates and terms when making major purchases (e.g., credit cards, automobiles, mortgages)!

10. Understand what depreciating assets are!

I hope you have enjoyed my first attempt at writing a book and becoming a published author. Furthermore, I hope you have found something in the book that makes your financial life easier. Lastly, I pray that you use common sense when dealing with your finances because, after all, common sense ain't common. It is indeed uncommon but can be learned through adversity, perseverance and an enduring positive attitude!